AI FOR BUSINESS

BOOST YOUR BUSINESS WITH SMART TOOLS

DR. KHURSHID EQBAL

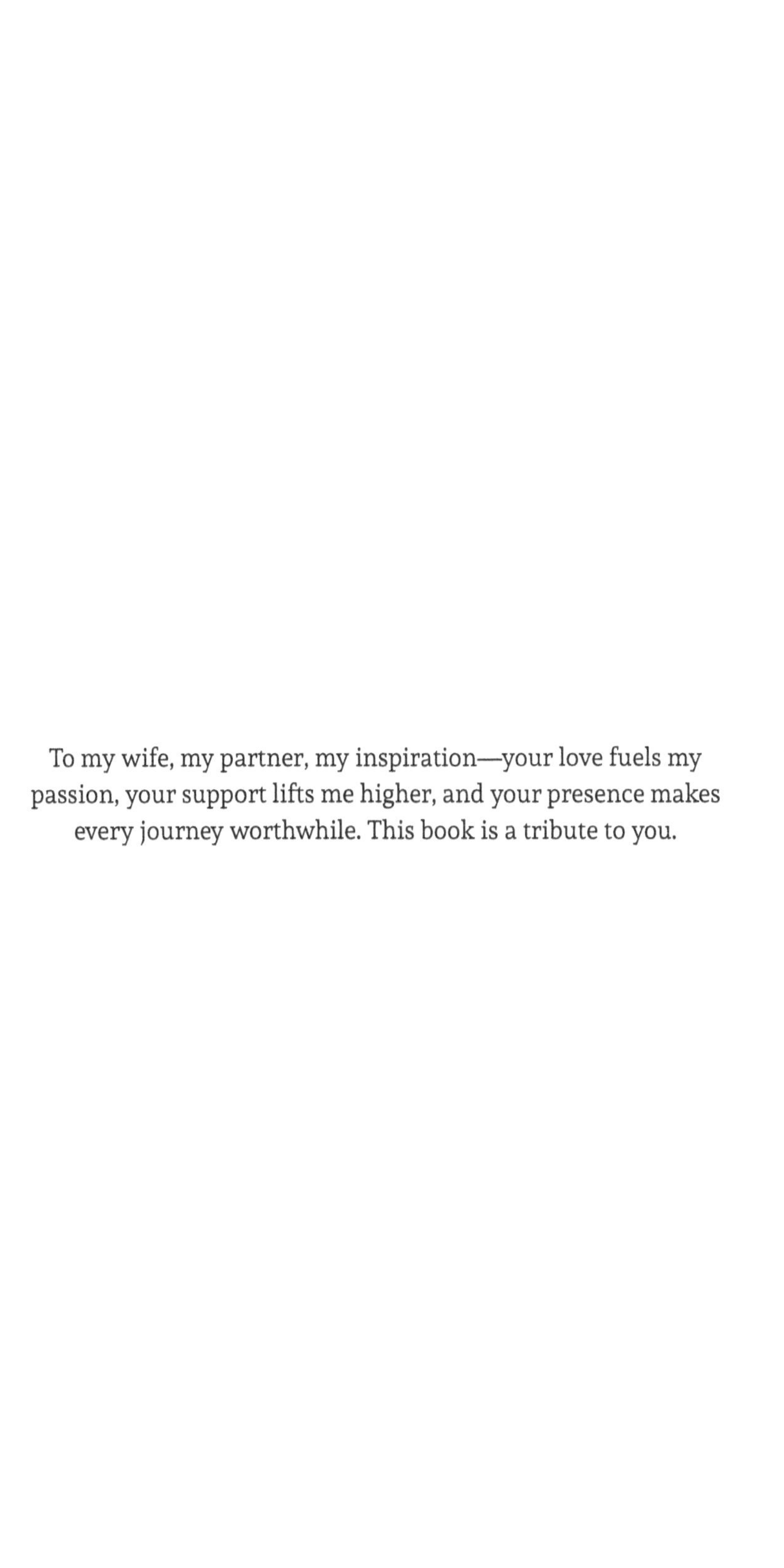

To my wife, my partner, my inspiration—your love fuels my passion, your support lifts me higher, and your presence makes every journey worthwhile. This book is a tribute to you.

Contents

Preface

Welcome to Your AI Adventure

When I sat down to write this book, I wasn't thinking about robots taking over the world or tech geniuses in lab coats. Nope — I was thinking about people like you and me. People who run coffee shops, sell handmade jewellery, deliver groceries, or dream of turning a side hustle into something big. People who don't have time for complicated tech talk but have a knack for spotting a good idea — one that saves time, cuts hassle, and piles up profits. That's what "AI in Business" is all about: showing you how Artificial Intelligence, or AI, isn't some sci-fi mystery — it's a real, ready-to-use tool that's already making businesses richer, easier, and more fun to run.

I'm not a coder or a scientist — I'm a writer who's watched the world change and seen how AI's gone from a buzzword to a game-changer. I've talked to shop owners who slashed waste with a simple app, managers who doubled sales with a smart trick, and entrepreneurs who found their footing with tools they grabbed off the internet. What hit me? You don't need a tech degree to win with AI — you just need to know it's there, waiting to help. So, I wrote this book for folks like us: non-techies who want practical, no-fuss ways to grow our businesses and bank accounts.

Why now? Because AI's not tomorrow's promise — it's today's power. Companies big and small —*Walmart* (https://www.walmart.com), *Zomato* (https://www.zomato.com), even the little saree shop down the street—are using it to save hours, charm customers, and cash in. I saw profits jump 20%, 30%, even 150% in some cases, all from ideas so simple you'll wonder why you didn't start sooner. This isn't a textbook — it's a roadmap, packed with stories, examples, and steps you can take right now, whether you're sipping chai at your desk or sketching plans on a napkin.

Here's what you'll find in these pages: ten chapters that walk you from "What's AI?" to "How do I start?" We'll see how it speeds up boring tasks (Chapter 2), keeps customers grinning (Chapter 3), supercharges sales (Chapter 4), streamlines making stuff (Chapter 5), masters money moves (Chapter 6), builds dream teams (Chapter 7), and delivers real wins (Chapter 8). Then, we'll peek into the future (Chapter 9) and hand you the keys to try it yourself (Chapter 10)—no geek glasses required. Every step's about profit—yours—because that's what business is for, right?

This book's for you if you're a shopkeeper tired of overstock, a manager juggling too many hats, or a dreamer ready to launch. It's for anyone who's thought, "There's got to be an easier way." Spoiler: there is, and AI's it. My goal? To leave you inspired, armed with tools like *Tidio* (https://www.tidio.com) or *Canva* (https://www.canva.com), and itching to see your own profits pop. No tech walls to climb—just a friendly nudge to grab what's yours.

Writing this was a blast — I've loved digging into these stories, imagining your wins, and keeping it real. As you flip through, picture your business—your coffee shop, your online store, your big idea — growing with every page. This isn't just my book — it's our adventure. So, let's dive in, start small, and cash in big. Your AI journey starts now—turn the page, and let's make some money together!

ONE

WHAT IS AI, AND WHY SHOULD YOU CARE?

Introduction: AI Isn't Just for Robots and Movies

Imagine you're running a small business—a cozy coffee shop on a busy street, a boutique selling handmade jewelry, or maybe a delivery service buzzing around town. You're juggling a dozen tasks: keeping track of stock, answering customer questions, figuring out what sells best, and somehow finding time to grow your profits. Now, what if you had a super-smart assistant who could handle half of that work for you—without ever needing a coffee break? That's what Artificial Intelligence, or AI, is all about. It's not some sci-fi mystery with robots taking over the world. It's a tool—practical, powerful, and already changing how businesses like yours make money.

In this chapter, we're going to peel back the curtain on AI. No tech degrees needed, no complicated terms—just plain talk about what it is, how it's already part of your life, and why you, yes YOU—a shop owner, a manager, or someone dreaming of starting a business—should care. Because here's the bottom line: AI isn't just for big companies with deep pockets. It's for anyone who wants to work smarter, save time, and see their profits climb. Let's dive in with a cup of chai and some simple ideas.

What is AI, Anyway? A Smart Helper, Not a Genius Robot

So, what exactly is AI? Think of it as a "smart assistant" that can look at information, spot patterns, and make decisions—faster and often better than a human could alone. It's like having an extra brain on your team, one that doesn't sleep, doesn't complain, and loves doing the boring stuff you hate. But don't worry—it's not here to replace you; it's here to make your life easier.

Here's an analogy you'll get right away: when you're texting your friend on your smartphone and it suggests the next word—like "great" after you type "that was a"—that's AI at work. It's watching what you type, guessing what's next, and saving you a few taps. It's not magic; it's just a tool trained to help. Now, imagine that same idea, but instead of texting, it's helping a business. Maybe it's predicting what products will sell out in your store or reminding customers to pay their bills—all without you lifting a finger. That's AI in a nutshell: a helper that learns from what it sees and does the heavy lifting for you.

AI in Your Everyday Life—It's Already Here!

You might think AI is some futuristic thing, but it's already all around you, working quietly in the background. Ever ordered something from *Amazon* and noticed how it suggests other stuff you might like? That's AI saying, "Hey, people who bought this also loved that!" Or maybe you've asked Google a question—like "What's the weather today?"—and it answers instantly. That's AI figuring out what you mean and digging up the info fast. Even when you're binge-watching on *Netflix* and it recommends a show you end up loving, guess what? Yup, AI again, watching your habits and picking winners.

For non-tech folks like us, this is the cool part: you don't need to know how it works under the hood. Just like you don't need to understand how a car engine runs to drive it, you don't need to code to use AI. Companies have already built these tools, and they're ready for you to plug into your business. The question isn't "Can I figure out AI?" It's "How can AI figure out my problems and make me more money?" And that's what we're here to explore.

Why Should You Care? Because It's About Time and Money

Okay, so AI is a smart assistant, and it's already in our lives. But why should YOU—a shop owner, a manager, or someone with a side hustle—care about it? Simple: it's about making your work easier and your profits bigger. Let's break it down.

First, **time**. Running a business is a race against the clock. You're counting inventory, chasing payments, or trying to guess what customers want next. AI steps in like a superhero sidekick and takes those headaches off your plate. It can do in seconds what might take you hours—like sorting through sales data to see what's hot or scheduling your staff so no one's overworked. More time means you can focus on the fun stuff: growing your business, dreaming up new ideas, or just relaxing with family instead of drowning in paperwork.

Second, **money**. Every minute AI saves you, it's also saving—or making—you cash. When you don't waste stock, miss deadlines, or lose customers because you're too busy to reply, your bottom line grows. AI isn't cheap because it's fancy; it's valuable because it cuts costs and boosts sales. Think of it as an investment that pays itself back, whether you're a big retailer or a one-person show.

A Quick Example: The Coffee Shop That Cracked the Code

Let's bring this home with a story. Picture Priya, who runs a small coffee shop called "Chai & Chill" in a bustling neighborhood. She's got loyal customers, but she's always scrambling—running out of cappuccino beans one day, overstocking iced lattes the next, and throwing away unsold pastries. Then she hears about an AI tool from her supplier. It's simple: she plugs in her sales numbers, and the AI tracks what's popular—say, cappuccinos sell like crazy on Mondays, but iced lattes tank in winter. It even predicts how much she'll sell next week based on weather and holidays.

Suddenly, Priya's not guessing anymore. She orders just enough beans, cuts waste by 30%, and starts offering discounts on slow days to bring people in. Her costs drop, her sales climb, and her profits? Up by a cool 20% in a month. She didn't need to code or hire a tech wizard—just used an app on her phone. That's AI doing its thing: turning chaos into cash, one coffee at a time.

The Big Picture: AI is Your Business Buddy

Here's the deal: AI isn't about replacing people or turning your business into a tech lab. It's about giving you an edge. Whether you're a tailor tracking fabric trends, a gym owner automating sign-ups, or a farmer figuring out when to plant, AI can help. It's like having a friend who's great with numbers and never forgets a detail—always there to spot opportunities and dodge mistakes.

Why should you care? Because the businesses using AI today—big ones like Walmart or local ones like Priya's shop—are pulling ahead. They're saving time, cutting costs, and raking in more profits. And the best part? You don't need to be a scientist to join them. This book is your roadmap—no tech talk, just real stories and ideas to show you how AI can work for YOU.

TWO

SPEEDING UP THE BASICS – AI IN DAILY OPERATIONS

Introduction: The Magic of Doing Less, Earning More

Let's face it—running a business is a lot like juggling flaming torches while riding a unicycle. You're keeping track of stock, planning deliveries, chasing payments, and somehow trying to smile through it all. Most days, you're stuck doing the same boring tasks over and over, wishing you had an extra pair of hands—or maybe ten. What if I told you there's a way to offload that grunt work, free up your time, and watch your profits grow? That's where Artificial Intelligence, or AI, steps in like a trusty sidekick, speeding up the basics so you can focus on the big wins.

In this chapter, we're diving into how AI automates the daily grind—those repetitive, time-sucking chores that every business deals with. We'll look at real examples, from a grocery store getting deliveries right to a gym sending payment reminders without lifting a finger. No tech talk here—just practical stories about how AI saves time, cuts costs, and puts more money in the bank. Whether you're a shop owner, a freelancer, or dreaming of your own startup, these are tasks you'll recognize—and solutions you can use. So, grab a snack, and let's see how AI makes the basics a breeze!

What Does "Speeding Up the Basics" Mean?

When we say "speeding up the basics," we're talking about all those must-do jobs that keep a business ticking but don't exactly light your fire. Think counting boxes in the backroom, figuring out when to reorder supplies, or calling customers to say, "Hey, your bill's due!" These tasks aren't glamorous, but they're the backbone of any operation. Problem is, they eat up hours—hours you could spend growing your business or, let's be honest, chilling with a *Netflix* binge.

AI is like hiring an assistant who's obsessed with details and never gets tired. It takes these repetitive jobs, does them faster than you ever could, and doesn't mess up. The best part? It's not just about saving time—it's about saving money and making more, too. Less time on boring stuff means more time for selling, creating, or just enjoying life. And when you're not wasting resources, your profits get a nice little boost. Let's walk through some examples to see how this works in the real world.

Example 1: Scheduling Deliveries Like a Pro – The Grocery Store Story

Meet Ravi, who runs a small grocery store called "Fresh Mart" in a busy suburb. Every week, he's got trucks rolling in with veggies, milk, and snacks, but figuring out when they should arrive is a headache. Too early, and his fridge overflows; too late, and customers walk away empty-handed. He used to spend hours guessing—checking old receipts, calling suppliers, stressing over traffic delays. Then he found an AI tool through his delivery app.

This tool looks at Ravi's sales—like how carrots sell out on weekends or milk flies off the shelves before holidays—and plans the deliveries automatically. It even checks weather forecasts (no point delivering tons of ice cream in a storm) and traffic updates to pick the perfect times. Now, deliveries show up just when he needs them, no overstocking, no shortages. Ravi saves two hours a week he used to spend planning, and his waste—those unsold, wilted veggies—drops by 25%. That's money straight back in his pocket, all because AI took over the scheduling. Could your deliveries use that kind of magic?

Example 2: Inventory That Minds Itself – The Clothing Brand Boost

Next up is Neha, who started a clothing brand called "Trendy Threads" selling kurtas and tees online. Her biggest nightmare? Inventory. She'd order too many red kurtas that didn't sell, then run out of blue tees everyone wanted. Counting stock by hand took half a day, and missteps meant lost sales or piles of leftovers she'd discount. Enter AI, via a simple app she found on *Shopify*.

This AI tracks what's selling—blue tees are hot in summer, red kurtas peak during Diwali—and predicts what she'll need next. It sends her a shopping list: "Order 50 blue tees, skip the red for now." It even flags slow movers, so she can push them with a sale before they gather dust. Neha's inventory time shrinks to 15 minutes a week, and her sales jump 30% because she's always got the right stuff. Less waste, more profit—AI turned her stockroom into a goldmine. Sound like something your business could use?

Example 3: Payment Reminders on Autopilot – The Gym That Never Forgets

Now, picture Arjun, who owns a small gym called "FitZone." He's got 50 members, but chasing late payments is a chore. Some forget, some dodge, and he's too nice to nag. He'd spend an hour every week texting or calling, "Hey, your fees are due!"—time he'd rather spend planning workouts. Then he tries an AI tool from his billing software.

This AI sends automatic reminders—polite texts like "Hi, your FitZone payment is due tomorrow!"—and tracks who's paid. If someone's late, it follows up with a friendly nudge, no awkward calls needed. Arjun's collection time drops to zero—he doesn't lift a finger—and late payments fall by 40%. That's extra cash flowing in, plus an hour back to tweak his Zumba class. Could your customers use a gentle nudge without you playing debt collector?

Real-World Big Player: How Amazon Predicts Your Next Buy

Let's zoom out to a giant you know: *Amazon* (https://www.*Amazon*.com). Ever wonder how they're so good at guessing what you'll buy next? That's AI running the show. When you order a book, AI looks at what millions of others bought with it—say, a bookmark or a coffee mug—and pops those up as "Frequently Bought Together." It's not random; it's AI spotting patterns in what people like you want.

For *Amazon*, this means less guesswork on what to stock in warehouses and more sales from spot-on suggestions. They save millions on unsold junk and make billions by keeping you clicking "Add to Cart." You don't need *Amazon*'s budget to do this—smaller tools can predict your customers' favorites too—but it shows how AI turns daily ops into profit machines.

How It Saves Time and Cuts Costs?

These stories have a common thread: AI takes tasks you'd slog through and zaps them into seconds. Scheduling deliveries? Done in a flash. Managing inventory? No sweat. Chasing payments? Handled. Here's the math:

- **Time Saved:** Hours a week turn into minutes. Ravi's two hours, Neha's half-day, Arjun's hour—all freed up for bigger things.
- **Costs Cut:** Less waste (Ravi's veggies, Neha's kurtas) and fewer missed sales mean money stays in your pocket.
- **Profits Up:** Smarter operations—like Arjun's extra fees or *Amazon*'s extra sales—grow your revenue without extra effort.

Think about your own day. What's that one task you dread—counting stock, sorting emails, planning shifts? AI can probably do it faster, cheaper, and better. It's like handing off the grunt work to a friend who's happy to help, leaving you to run the show.

Why This Matters to You?

You don't need to be a tech whiz to see the win here. These are tasks YOU might do—whether you're a baker tracking flour, a tutor scheduling classes, or a vendor juggling orders at a market. AI isn't about fancy gadgets; it's about taking the boring bits off your plate. And when you're not bogged down, you've got room to dream—maybe open a second shop, launch a new product, or just take a day off without chaos.

The profit boost isn't a pipe dream either. Businesses using AI for daily ops—like Ravi, Neha, and Arjun—see real gains: 20%, 30%, even 40% more in their bank accounts. It's not about replacing people; it's about making your team (even if it's just you!) more efficient. Less manual work, more money—it's that simple.

THREE

HAPPY CUSTOMERS, HAPPY PROFITS – AI IN CUSTOMER SERVICE

Introduction: The Secret Sauce to Keeping Customers Coming Back

Imagine this: you walk into your favorite café, and the barista already knows you want a caramel latte—extra foam, no sugar—before you even open your mouth. You feel special, right? That little touch keeps you coming back, maybe even tipping extra. Now, what if your business could do that for every customer, all day, every day, without breaking a sweat? That's where Artificial Intelligence, or AI, comes in—it's like giving your customers a VIP experience, and in return, they reward you with loyalty and bigger profits.

In this chapter, we're diving into how AI transforms customer service from a headache into a goldmine. No tech degree needed—just simple ideas about how AI answers questions, suggests products, and keeps people happy, all while boosting your sales. We'll meet a travel website that never sleeps, an online store like *Flipkart* that knows what you want, and a restaurant owner who turned one-time diners into regulars. For shop owners, managers, or anyone with a hustle, this is about making customers love you—and watching your profits soar. Let's get started with a smile and some real-world wins!

Why Customer Service Matters (And How AI Makes It Better)?

Here's a truth every business owner knows: happy customers are your bread and butter. If they're smiling, they're buying—and telling their friends to buy too. But keeping them happy? That's tough. Phone calls pile up, emails go unanswered, and one grumpy customer can ruin your day. AI steps in like a superhero, handling the chaos so you don't have to. It's not about replacing your charm; it's about giving you tools to shine brighter.

Think of AI as your 24/7 customer service champ. It doesn't sleep, doesn't get cranky, and can talk to ten people at once without missing a beat. Whether it's answering questions, solving problems, or suggesting the perfect product, AI makes sure your customers feel heard and cared for. And here's the kicker: when they're happy, they spend more and come back again. That's the magic link—great service equals bigger profits. Let's see how this plays out with some everyday examples.

Example 1: Chatbots That Never Sleep – The Travel Website Win

Meet Priya, who runs "WanderEasy," a small travel website booking trips to hill stations and beaches. Her customers love browsing late at night, but Priya can't stay up answering questions like "Is the Manali package pet-friendly?" or "What's the cancellation policy?" She used to lose sales because people wouldn't wait till morning.

Then she added a chatbot—an AI helper—from a tool like *Tidio*.

This chatbot works round the clock, chatting with visitors like a friendly guide. "Yes, pets are welcome in Manali—here's the package!" or "Cancel up to 24 hours before, no charge—book now?" It's fast, polite, and always on. Priya's customers get answers instantly, so they book instead of bouncing. Her bookings jump 35%—that's hundreds of extra rupees a month—and she sleeps easy knowing her site's covered. Could your business use a night-shift buddy like that?

Example 2: Smart Suggestions That Sell – The Flipkart Trick

Now, let's talk about *Flipkart* (https://www.flipkart.com), India's online shopping giant. Ever notice how when you buy a phone, it suggests a case or earbuds right below? That's AI at work, playing matchmaker with products. It looks at what you're buying, what others bought with it, and says, "Hey, you might like this too!" It's not random—it's smart, like a shop assistant who knows your taste.

For *Flipkart*, this means more sales per customer. You came for a phone but leave with a whole kit—boom, profit up. Smaller businesses can do this too. Imagine you sell handmade soaps online. An AI tool could suggest a lavender scrub with every rose soap order, nudging buyers to spend a bit more. It's effortless, and those extra sales add up fast. Ever thought about suggesting the perfect add-on to your customers?

Example 3: Personalized Discounts That Hook – The Restaurant Comeback

Here's a tasty story: Sanjay owns "Spice Haven," a cozy restaurant famous for biryani. He's got decent footfall, but he wants regulars, not just one-time eaters. He starts using an AI tool from his email software to send personalized offers. It looks at what customers ordered—like who loves spicy chicken or who's a veg thali fan—and crafts discounts just for them.

One day, it emails Ravi, a guy who ordered chicken biryani twice last month: "Hey Ravi, 20% off your next biryani this weekend!" Ravi's thrilled—he feels noticed—and comes back, bringing friends. Sanjay's repeat business climbs 40%, and his profits spike because those regulars keep the cash flowing. No tech skills needed—just an AI that knows Sanjay's customers better than he does. Could a little personalization bring your customers back too?

How AI Makes Customers Happy (And Profits Happier)?

These stories show AI doing three big things for customer service:

1. **Always There:** Chatbots like Priya's mean no one waits — day or night, answers are instant. Happy customers don't walk away; they buy.
2. **Spot-On Suggestions:** Flipkart's AI turns browsers into spenders by guessing what they'll love next. More items per cart, more money per sale.
3. **Personal Touch:** Sanjay's discounts make customers feel special, not just another order number. That connection means loyalty — and repeat profits.

Here's the payoff:

- **Time Saved:** No more late-night calls or endless email chains—AI handles it, freeing you up.
- **Costs Down:** Fewer staff hours on service means lower overhead, especially for small businesses.
- **Sales Up:** Happy customers spend more and come back, turning one sale into ten.

Think about your own customers. How many leave because they can't get help fast? Or don't buy more because they don't know what else you've got? AI fixes that, and your bank account thanks you.

Why This Matters to You?

You don't need to be a big shot to care about this. Whether you're a travel agent like Priya, an online seller like Flipkart, or a local eatery like Sanjay, customer service is your lifeline. AI makes it easier to keep people happy without burning out. It's like having a team member who's all about "yes"— yes to quick replies, yes to smart ideas, yes to keeping customers smiling.

And the profit part? It's real. Priya's 35% booking boost, Flipkart's extra sales, Sanjay's 40% repeat business — these aren't flukes. Happy customers don't just pay once; they pay again and again, spreading the word too. You don't need a tech degree to tap into this — just a willingness to let AI handle the heavy lifting while you reap the rewards.

A Peek Behind the Curtain (No Tech Talk, Promise!)

How does AI do this? Picture it like a super-observant friend. It watches what customers do—what they ask, what they buy, what they skip—and learns from it. Chatbots "listen" to questions and pull answers from a list you give them. Suggestions come from spotting patterns, like "phone buyers love cases." Discounts use past orders to guess what'll tempt someone back. It's not magic—it's just a tool doing what you'd do if you had infinite time and a perfect memory.

FOUR

Selling Smarter – AI in Marketing and Sales

Introduction: Turning Guesses into Gold

Picture this: you're running a small jewellery shop, and you've got a stunning new collection of silver bangles. You could blast ads to everyone in town, hoping someone bites, or you could magically know exactly who's itching to buy them—say, young women planning for a wedding season. What if you had a tool that not only found those perfect customers but also told you how to win them over? That's Artificial Intelligence, or AI, stepping into the world of marketing and sales, turning your wild guesses into a treasure chest of profits.

In this chapter, we're exploring how AI helps businesses—big and small—sell smarter, not harder. It's about targeting the right people, at the right time, with the right stuff, without wasting a dime on shots in the dark. We'll see how *Netflix* nails show recommendations, how a jewellery shop zeroes in on buyers, and how a shoe brand spots trends to sell out fast. For shop owners, entrepreneurs, or anyone who's ever sold a thing, this is your ticket to more sales and bigger profits—no tech wizardry required. Let's dive in and see how AI flips the sales game on its head!

Why Selling Smarter Matters?

Selling isn't just about having a great product—it's about getting it into the hands of people who'll love it. The old way? Throw ads everywhere—billboards, emails, social media—and pray something sticks. It's like tossing spaghetti at a wall and hoping it holds. Problem is, that wastes time and money, and half your customers never even see it. AI changes all that. It's like having a super-smart salesperson who knows exactly who's buying, what they want, and how to hook them.

Here's the deal: AI looks at what people do—clicks, likes, purchases—and figures out who's your golden ticket. It cuts through the noise, so your marketing hits the bullseye every time. Less waste, more wins. And when you sell more with less effort, your profits don't just creep up—they leap. Whether you're a giant like *Amazon* or a one-person hustle, AI makes selling a breeze. Let's break it down with some real-world magic.

Example 1: Recommendations That Reel You In – The Netflix Play

You've probably been sucked into a *Netflix* binge, right? One minute you're watching a crime drama, and next thing you know, it's suggesting a thriller that's *exactly* your vibe. That's AI playing Cupid with your screen time. It watches what you watch, how long you stick around, and what others like you enjoy—then bam, it picks the perfect next show.

For *Netflix*, this isn't just fun—it's profit. Every recommendation keeps you hooked, renewing that subscription month after month. They've turned guessing into a science, boosting watch time by 20% (that's millions of hours!), which means more money without making a single extra show. Imagine your business doing that—suggesting a scarf with every saree or a dessert with every meal, nudging customers to spend more. AI's got that knack, and it's a sales goldmine.

Example 2: Targeting the Right Buyers – The Jewellery Shop Jackpot

Let's meet Priya again — this time, she's running "Silver Sparkle," a jewellery shop with a shiny new collection of bangles. She used to send flyers to everyone in her city, but half her mail ended up in the trash — costly and pointless. Then she tries an AI tool from her *Facebook* ads dashboard. It digs into who's clicking her posts — mostly women aged 25-35, often liking wedding pages or gift ideas — and targets them with ads: "Wedding-ready bangles, 10% off this week!"

Suddenly, Priya's not shouting into the void. Her ads hit the right eyes, and sales spike 40% in a month — she's selling 50 bangles instead of 30, all for less ad spend. No tech degree needed — just an AI that knows her customers better than she does. Could your business find its perfect crowd like that?

Example 3: Spotting Trends to Sell Big – The Shoe Brand Surge

Now, picture Vikram, who owns "StepUp Shoes," a small brand selling trendy sneakers online. He's got a hunch neon colors are hot, but he's not sure. He used to order stock based on gut feelings — sometimes winning, sometimes stuck with unsold piles. Then he uses an AI tool from *Instagram* that scans social media buzz. It spots hashtags like #NeonVibes trending with teens, plus tons of likes on bright shoe pics.

Vikram doubles down — orders neon sneakers, launches a campaign: "Glow up your step!"— and sells out in two weeks. Sales jump 50%, and he's not stuck with flops. AI didn't just guess; it "knew" what customers wanted, cutting waste and driving revenue. Ever wondered what your customers are buzzing about? AI's got the scoop.

How AI Makes Marketing and Sales Smarter?

These stories show AI doing three killer moves:

1. **Perfect Picks:** Like *Netflix*, it suggests stuff customers can't resist, turning one sale into two or three.
2. **Laser Targeting:** Priya's AI finds the right buyers, so every ad rupee counts—no more spaghetti-on-the-wall chaos.
3. **Trend Tracking:** Vikram's AI sniffs out what's hot, letting you ride the wave before it crashes.

Here's the payoff:

- **Time Saved:** No more endless ad tweaks or trend hunts — AI does it in minutes.
- **Costs Cut:** Less wasted marketing means more budget for what works.
- **Revenue Up:** Smarter sales — *Netflix*'s subscriptions, Priya's bangles, Vikram's sneakers — mean bigger profits fast.

Think about your own sales. Are you guessing who'll buy? Wasting cash on ads that flop? AI turns that around, making every move a money-maker.

Why This Matters to You?

You don't need a marketing degree or a tech team to care about this. Whether you're selling bangles like Priya, shoes like Vikram, or subscriptions like *Netflix*, AI's your secret weapon. It's like having a sales guru who never sleeps—finding customers, pitching products, and spotting trends while you sip your chai. And it's not just for big shots; small businesses can grab affordable tools from Google Ads or *Facebook* to play the same game.

The profit boost is real. Priya's 40%, Vikram's 50%, *Netflix*'s millions — these aren't fairy tales. Smarter selling means more sales with less effort, and that's cash in your pocket. You don't need to code or crunch numbers — just let AI do the heavy lifting and watch your business grow.

A Peek Behind the Curtain (No Tech Talk, Promise!)

How does AI pull this off? Imagine it's your nosiest friend—always watching, always learning. It sees what people click on *Instagram*, what they buy on *Flipkart*, what they search on *Google* — then connects the dots. Recommendations? It's like "Hey, they loved this, they'll love that." Targeting? It's "These folks keep clicking jewelry—show 'em more!" Trends? It's "Neon's blowing up—stock it now!" It's not brain surgery—it's just a tool that's really good at paying attention.

FIVE

MAKING STUFF EASIER – AI IN MANUFACTURING AND SUPPLY CHAINS

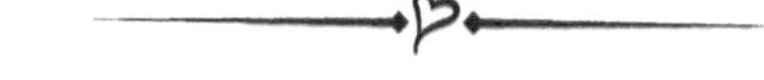

Introduction: Turning Chaos into Cash

Imagine you're running a toy factory, churning out plastic robots and dolls, or maybe you're hustling packages across town for a delivery gig. One day, you make too many toys that don't sell; the next, you're scrambling because you didn't make enough. Deliveries? Either your trucks are stuck in traffic or burning fuel on half-empty runs. It's a mess—stressful, costly, and a profit killer. What if you had a secret weapon that could predict what's needed, plan smarter, and keep everything humming along? That's Artificial Intelligence, or AI, stepping in to make making and moving stuff a whole lot easier.

In this chapter, we're diving into how AI takes the headache out of manufacturing and supply chains—the nuts and bolts of getting products made and delivered. No tech talk here—just real stories about a toy factory nailing demand, a delivery giant like *FedEx* saving fuel, and how this all means more money in your pocket. Whether you're a factory owner, a logistics pro, or just someone who sells stuff, this is about cutting waste, speeding things up, and boosting profits. Let's roll up our sleeves and see how AI turns chaos into cash!

Why Manufacturing and Supply Chains Need a Boost?

Making stuff and getting it to customers is the backbone of tons of businesses—think toys, clothes, food, you name it. But it's tricky. In manufacturing, you've got to guess how much to make—too much, and you're stuck with junk no one wants; too little, and you miss sales. Supply chains? That's moving those goods—planning routes, dodging delays, keeping costs low. Get it wrong, and you're bleeding money on extra storage, late shipments, or wasted fuel.

Here's where AI comes in like a sharp-eyed foreman. It spots patterns humans miss—like what sells when, or the fastest way from A to B—and makes the whole process smoother. It's not about fancy robots welding cars (though it can do that too); it's about practical help for everyday challenges. Less downtime, less waste, more profit—that's the promise. Let's see how this plays out with some real-world wins.

Example 1: Predicting Demand Like a Pro – The Toy Factory Triumph

Meet Anjali, who runs "PlayPal Toys," a small factory making plastic robots and dolls. Every Christmas, she's sweating bullets—will kids want robots this year, or dolls? Last year, she overdid the robots, and half sat unsold; the year before, dolls ran out, and she lost orders. Guessing was costing her big—hours planning, money on extra stock, and missed sales. Then she tries an AI tool from her supplier's app.

This AI looks at her sales—robots spike in November, dolls peak in December—plus stuff like toy trends online and weather (rainy days mean more indoor play). It says, "Make 5,000 robots by October, 7,000 dolls by November." Anjali follows the plan, and boom—stock matches demand perfectly. No overstock, no shortages. She cuts production waste by 20% (that's thousands of rupees saved) and boosts sales 30% by never running out. Planning time? Down from days to minutes. Could your business predict a hit like that?

Example 2: Routes That Save Fuel – The FedEx Formula

Now, let's zoom to *FedEx*, the delivery giant moving packages worldwide. Fuel's a monster expense—trucks crisscrossing cities, sometimes half-empty or stuck in jams. They used to rely on drivers' know-how and basic maps, but that wasn't enough. Enter AI, built into their routing system.

This AI crunches everything—traffic patterns, package sizes, delivery deadlines—and maps the smartest routes. "Take Main Street at 10 a.m., avoid the market at noon," it says, packing trucks full and cutting detours. FedEx shaves 20 million miles off its routes yearly—that's millions in fuel saved—and delivers faster, keeping customers happy. Smaller players can do this too—an AI app could tell your delivery guy the best path, slashing costs. Ever thought about saving fuel while speeding up?

Example 3: Smarter Stocking – The Grocery Chain Glow-Up

Here's Vikram, who manages "FreshBazaar," a chain of three grocery stores. Stocking's a nightmare—too many mangoes rot, too few eggs mean angry customers. He'd spend hours juggling orders, often wrong. Then he uses an AI tool from *Walmart's* playbook, tweaked for his size.

This AI tracks sales—eggs fly out Monday mornings, mangoes slow midweek—plus local events (a festival means more sweets). It tells Vikram, "Order 200 eggs Sunday, 50 mangoes Wednesday." Stock stays fresh, shelves stay full. Waste drops 25%, and sales rise 15% because he's got what people want. No more late-night math—just AI doing the heavy lifting. Could your stockroom use that kind of smarts?

How AI Makes It All Easier?

These stories show AI working three big tricks:

1. **Demand Prediction:** Anjali's AI knows what'll sell, so she makes just enough—no excess, no misses.
2. **Route Optimization:***FedEx's* AI cuts miles and fuel, speeding up deliveries with less cost.
3. **Stock Precision:** Vikram's AI keeps shelves perfect, slashing waste and boosting sales.

Here's the payoff:

- **Time Saved**: Planning drops from hours (or days) to minutes—Anjali's not guessing, Vikram's not stressing.
- **Costs Cut:** Less waste (toys, food) and fuel mean money stays in the bank—20-25% savings add up.
- **Profits Up:** Smarter moves—more sales, faster deliveries—lift revenue 15-30% without extra work.

Think about your own grind. Overstocked lately? Lost time on bad routes? AI's like a crystal ball and GPS rolled into one—spotting what's next and getting it there cheap.

Why This Matters to You?

You don't need a factory or a fleet to care about this. Whether you're making candles at home, shipping handmade soaps, or running a food stall, manufacturing and supply chains touch you. AI's not just for big guns like *FedEx*—small fries like Anjali and Vikram use it too, with tools from apps or suppliers. It's about working less to make more, cutting the fat, and keeping things rolling.

The profit gains are real. Anjali's 30%, Vikram's 15%, *FedEx's* millions — these aren't flukes. Less downtime (no idle machines), less waste (no unsold stock), smarter planning (no lost deliveries)—it all stacks up to cash. You don't need to know tech — just plug in AI and watch it pay off.

A Peek Behind the Curtain (No Tech Talk, Promise!)

How does AI do this? Think of it as your eagle-eyed buddy. It watches sales (robots vs. dolls), tracks maps (traffic jams), checks trends (egg rush Mondays)—then calls the shots. Prediction? "Kids want this now." Routes? "Go this way, save gas." Stock? "Order this much, no more." It's not rocket science—it's just a tool that's great at connecting dots you'd miss.

SIX

MONEY MATTERS – AI IN FINANCE AND DECISION-MAKING

Introduction: Your Money's New Best Friend

Picture yourself juggling the cash side of your business—counting sales, dodging scams, guessing next month's bills. One wrong move, and you're either broke or missing a golden chance. It's like playing chess blindfolded—stressful, risky, and way too easy to mess up. What if you had a sharp-eyed partner who could crunch numbers, spot trouble, and make smart calls faster than you can say "profit"? That's Artificial Intelligence, or AI, stepping in to take the guesswork out of money matters.

In this chapter, we're digging into how AI handles finances and decisions better than us mere mortals. No calculators or tech degrees needed—just real stories about a bank catching crooks, a bakery nailing its sales forecast, and a startup budgeting like a pro. Whether you're a café owner, a freelancer, or dreaming of your own gig, this is about cutting mistakes, saving cash, and growing profits with AI as your money buddy. Let's crack open the piggy bank and see how it works!

Why Money and Decisions Are Tricky (And How AI Helps)?

Money's the lifeblood of any business, big or small. You've got to track it, protect it, and figure out where it's going next—easy to say, tough to do. Ever misjudged a busy week and run out of stock? Or missed a sneaky scam that drained your account? Decisions matter too—when to spend, when to save, what risks to take. Get it wrong, and you're counting losses instead of gains.

AI's like a super-smart accountant and advisor rolled into one. It crunches numbers without breaking a sweat, spots patterns you'd never see, and makes choices faster than you can blink. It's not about replacing your gut—it's about giving you a crystal-clear view so your gut calls are winners. Less oops moments, more smart moves—that's how AI turns money matters into profit makers. Let's dive into some examples to see it in action.

Example 1: Catching Fraud Before It Hurts – The Bank's AI Shield

Meet Priya, who manages a small community bank, "People's Trust." She's proud of her customers, but fraud's a constant worry—fake transactions, stolen cards, sneaky thieves. One day, a scammer slips through, siphoning INR 50,000 before she catches it. Chasing it down takes hours, and the loss stings. Then she hooks up an AI tool from her banking software.

This AI watches every transaction—INR 500 here, INR 5,000 there—and flags anything fishy. "This guy's spending in Delhi and Mumbai same day—hold up!" it says, freezing the card before more damage hits. It learns from past scams too, getting sharper every time. Priya cuts fraud losses by 80%—that's lakhs saved yearly—and her customers trust her more, keeping their accounts active. No tech skills needed—just AI playing guard dog. Could your cash use that kind of shield?

Example 2: Forecasting Sales Like a Crystal Ball – The Bakery Boom

Next up is Sanjay, who runs "Sweet Rise Bakery," a cozy spot for cakes and bread. He's always guessing—how many cupcakes for Saturday? Too many, and they're trash; too few, and customers grumble. Last Holi, he baked 100 extra, but sold 50—half went stale, costing him INR 2,000. Then he tries an AI app from his point-of-sale system.

This AI looks at his sales—cupcakes spike weekends, bread dips midweek—plus holidays, weather (rain means more tea buns), even local events. "Bake 150 cupcakes Saturday, 80 bread Tuesday," it says. Sanjay nails it—sells out without waste. His planning time drops from an hour to minutes, waste falls 30%, and sales climb 25% because he's ready for the rush. That's extra dough in his pocket—literally. Ever wished you could predict your busy days?

Example 3: Budgeting Wisely – The Startup's Smart Start

Now, picture Neha, who's launching "Crafty Corner," a startup selling handmade candles online. Cash is tight—she's got INR 50,000 to start, and every rupee counts. Should she spend on ads, stock, or shipping? Guessing wrong could sink her. She grabs an AI tool from *QuickBooks* (www.quickbooks.intuit.com), a simple app for small fries like her.

This AI tracks her early sales—lavender candles sell fast, vanilla lags—plus costs like wax and wicks. It says, "Spend INR 20,000 on lavender stock, INR 10,000 on ads, save the rest." Neha follows it, doubles her sales in a month, and avoids blowing cash on slow movers. Mistakes drop to zero, and her profit's up 20% because she's spending smart. No finance degree—just AI keeping her on track. Could your budget use a little wisdom?

Relatable Scenario: The Café Owner's Coffee Call

Let's bring it home. Imagine you're Arjun, running "Bean Bliss Café." You're low on coffee beans—should you order more now or wait? Last month, you waited, ran out, and lost INR 5,000 in sales. You try an AI tool from your supplier's app. It checks your sales—beans fly out Mondays, slow Fridays—plus weather (hot days mean iced coffee). "Order 10 kilos now, skip next week," it says. You do, serve every customer, and save INR 1,000 on extra shipping. Sales hold steady, profits nudge up 15%. No late-night math—just AI making the call. Sound like your kind of helper?

How AI Handles Numbers and Choices?

These stories show AI pulling off three big wins:

1. **Fraud Busting:** Priya's AI spots trouble fast, saving cash and trust—no losses, just gains.
2. **Sales Forecasting:** Sanjay's AI predicts demand, cutting waste and boosting sales—perfect planning, perfect profits.
3. **Budget Smarts:** Neha's AI picks winners, dodging flops—every rupee works harder.

Here's the payoff:

- **Time Saved:** Hours of number-crunching shrink to minutes—Priya's not chasing, Sanjay's not guessing.
- **Mistakes Down:** No fraud slips, no overstock, no budget blunders—80% less loss, 30% less waste.
- **Profits Up:** Smarter calls—25% more sales, 20% better margins—mean money piles up fast.

Think about your own numbers. Lose sleep over scams? Miss a sales rush? AI's like a hawk-eyed accountant—watching, planning, winning.

Why This Matters to You?

You don't need to be a banker or math whiz to care. Whether you're guarding cash like Priya, forecasting like Sanjay, budgeting like Neha, or just picking beans like Arjun, money matters touch you. AI's not for Wall Street alone—small businesses grab tools from *QuickBooks (https://www.quickbooks.intuit.com)* or suppliers to play the same game. It's about fewer oops, more aha—less risk, more reward.

The profit boost is real. Priya's 80% fraud cut, Sanjay's 25% sales lift, Neha's 20% gain—these stack up. Less mistakes (no losses), smarter choices (more sales)—it's cash in hand. You don't need to crunch numbers—just let AI do it and cash the check.

A Peek Behind the Curtain (No Tech Talk, Promise!)

How's AI so good at this? Think of it as your eagle-eyed pal. It watches transactions (fraud flags), sales (busy days), costs (what's worth it)—then decides. Fraud? "That's odd—stop it!" Forecasts? "Sell this much Tuesday." Budgets? "Spend here, save there." It's not wizardry—it's just a tool that's ace at numbers and choices, like you with infinite time.

SEVEN

Hiring and Helping – AI in Human Resources

Introduction: Your HR Buddy That Never Sleeps

Running a business is all about people—finding the right ones to hire, keeping them happy, and building a team that rocks. But let's be real: sorting through a pile of resumes feels like digging for gold in a haystack, and figuring out if your crew's smiling or secretly plotting to quit? That's a whole other headache. What if you had a trusty sidekick who could zip through those tasks, spot the best hires, and keep your team humming—all without a coffee break? That's Artificial Intelligence, or AI, stepping in as your HR buddy.

In this chapter, we're diving into how AI makes hiring and managing people a breeze. No tech know-how needed—just fun, practical stories about a retail chain nabbing cashiers fast, a café tracking happiness to cut turnover, and how this all builds better teams that make more money. Whether you're a shop owner, a manager, or a solo entrepreneur with big dreams, this is about saving time, dodging drama, and boosting profits with AI as your people-whisperer. Let's grab a chai and see how it works!

Why HR Needs a Little Help (And How AI Delivers)?

People are your business's heartbeat—cashiers, cooks, drivers, you name it. But hiring them? It's a slog—hours reading resumes, guessing who'll show up on time. Managing them? Even trickier—keeping them happy, spotting burnout, making sure they stick around. Mess it up, and you're stuck with empty shifts, grumpy teams, and profits leaking out the door.

AI's like your HR fairy godmother—lightening the load so you can focus on running the show. It sorts resumes faster than you can say "interview," finds the perfect fits, and even keeps an eye on how your team's feeling. It's not about replacing your gut—it's about giving you a turbo boost to hire smart and help better. Less chaos, stronger crews, bigger bucks—that's the game plan. Let's roll through some real-life wins to see how it plays out.

Example 1: Sorting Resumes Like a Champ – The Retail Chain Rescue

Meet Ravi, who manages "ShopSmart," a retail chain with five stores. He needs cashiers fast—holiday rush is coming, and he's down three people. Normally, he'd spend days drowning in 100 resumes, half from folks who can't count change. Then he tries an AI tool from *Indeed* (https://www.indeed.com), a job site he already uses.

This AI scans every resume in seconds—checks skills (cash handling, customer service), flags red flags (gaps, no-shows), and picks the top 10 fits. "Ravi, these folks worked registers before—call them!" it says. He interviews five, hires three on the spot—all stars. Hiring time drops from a week to a day, and his stores stay staffed. No tech fuss—just AI playing matchmaker. Could your next hire be that easy?

Example 2: Tracking Happiness to Keep the Team – The Café Comeback

Now, picture Priya, who runs "Bean Bliss Café." Her baristas are great, but lately, two quit—no warning, just gone. Turnover's a killer—training newbies costs INR 10,000 each time, and grumpy staff scare off customers. She grabs an AI tool from *Workplace* (https://www.workplace.com), a team app she's got.

This AI checks in—sends quick surveys like "Happy with your shifts?" or "Need a break?"—and spots trouble. "Priya, Amit's stressed—talk to him," it flags. She chats, tweaks his hours, and he stays. Turnover drops 50%—that's INR 20,000 saved yearly—and her café's vibe lifts, pulling in 15% more sales from happy regulars. No HR degree—just AI keeping the peace. Ever wondered why your team's quiet lately?

Example 3: Smarter Scheduling – The Delivery Crew Boost

Here's Vikram, who owns "FastFeet Delivery," a small crew dropping off groceries. Scheduling's a nightmare—too many drivers one day, too few the next. Last month, he overstaffed, wasting INR 5,000; the next, he missed deliveries, losing INR 3,000. He tries an AI tool from his *Google Workspace* (https://workspace.google.com).

This AI looks at orders—busy Mondays, slow Thursdays—plus traffic and weather. "Schedule three drivers Monday, one Thursday," it says. Vikram nails it—no overtime, no missed drops. Scheduling time shrinks from an hour to minutes, costs fall 20%, and on-time deliveries jump 30%, earning him more gigs. That's profit ticking up without the hassle. Could your crew use that kind of rhythm?

How AI Makes HR Easier?

These stories show AI pulling off three slick moves:

1. **Hiring Fast:** Ravi's AI sorts resumes like a pro, finding gems quick—less digging, more doing.
2. **Happiness Check:** Priya's AI keeps tabs on team vibes, cutting turnover—happy crew, happy cash flow.
3. **Schedule Smarts:** Vikram's AI plans shifts right, saving cash and stress—smooth ops, sweet profits.

Here's the payoff:

- **Time Saved:** Days of hiring or scheduling shrink to minutes—Ravi's week, Priya's chats, Vikram's hour, gone.
- **Costs Cut:** Less turnover (50% down), less waste (20% off)—that's INR 20,000+ saved yearly.
- **Profits Up:** Better teams—15-30% more sales—mean money rolls in steady.

Think about your people. Drowning in resumes? Losing staff? AI's your HR buddy—hiring fast, helping smart.

Why This Matters to You?

You don't need to be an HR guru to care. Whether you're hiring cashiers like Ravi, keeping baristas like Priya, or scheduling drivers like Vikram, people stuff touches you. AI's not just for corporate suits—small fries grab tools from *Indeed* (https://www.indeed.com) or *Google* (https://www.google.com) to play the game. It's about less hassle, better teams, and more cash—no clipboard required.

The profit boost is real. Priya's 15%, Vikram's 30%, Ravi's smooth rush—these pile up. Less turnover (no training costs), better hires (no flops)—it's money in the bank. You don't need to crunch HR stats—just let AI handle it and watch your business shine.

A Peek Behind the Curtain (No Tech Talk, Promise!)

How's AI so slick at this? Picture it as your eagle-eyed pal. It scans resumes (skills, fit), watches vibes (surveys, flags), tracks patterns (busy days)—then acts. Hiring? "These are your stars." Happiness? "Fix this now." Schedules? "Here's the plan." It's not wizardry—it's a tool that's ace at people puzzles, like you with endless time.

EIGHT

REAL STORIES – COMPANIES WINNING WITH AI

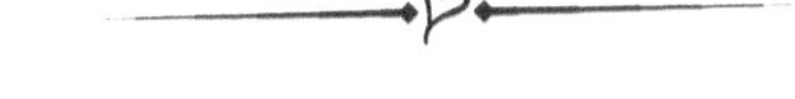

Introduction: Proof in the Profits

So far, we've talked about how AI can speed up your work, charm your customers, boost your sales, streamline your stuff, crunch your numbers, and build your team. But maybe you're thinking, "Sounds great, but does it really work in the real world?" Oh, it does—and this chapter's here to prove it. We're pulling back the curtain on companies—big, medium, and small—who've grabbed AI by the horns and turned it into cold, hard cash.

In these pages, you'll meet giants like *Walmart* (https://www.walmart.com), Indian champs like *Zomato* (https://www.zomato.com), and a little shop next door, all winning big with AI. No tech mumbo-jumbo—just stories of how they used simple tools to save time, cut costs, and pile up profits. Whether you're a shop owner, a manager, or dreaming of your own gig, these tales will light a fire under you—showing what's possible when AI's on your side. Grab a snack, and let's dive into some real-world wins!

Why Real Stories Matter?

Ideas are cool, but results? That's where the rubber meets the road. Seeing AI in action—how it's already making businesses richer—makes it real, not just a "what if." These aren't fairy tales; they're companies you know or could be, using AI to solve problems you've probably faced. From stocking shelves to delivering food to posting ads, these stories show the profit punch AI packs. Big names bring the wow, midsize firms show the hustle, and small shops prove you don't need a fortune to start. Let's meet the winners!

Case Study 1: Walmart – The Inventory King

First up, *Walmart* (https://www.walmart.com) — the retail giant with stores everywhere, selling everything from toothpaste to TVs. With millions of products moving daily, inventory's their lifeline. Too much stock clogs warehouses; too little leaves shelves bare. They used to rely on human guesswork—good, but not perfect. Then they plugged AI into their system.

This AI tracks sales—diapers fly out in baby boom towns, grills spike in summer—plus weather, holidays, even local events. "Stock 10,000 diapers in Delhi, 500 grills in Mumbai," it says, predicting demand down to the store. It also flags slow movers—say, winter coats in May—for quick discounts. Result? Walmart cuts inventory waste by 20%—that's millions saved yearly—and boosts sales 15% by always having what customers want. Downtime? Slashed—shelves stay full, cash keeps flowing. A big player, sure, but the lesson's simple: AI keeps stock smart, profits fat.

Case Study 2: Zomato – The Delivery Dynamo

Next, let's roll into India with *Zomato* (https://www.zomato.com), the food delivery champ serving biryani and pizzas to millions. Speed's their game—late orders mean grumpy eaters and lost tips.

They've got riders zipping through cities, but traffic, rain, and order spikes can throw a wrench in the works. Enter AI, baked into their app.

This AI maps it all—traffic jams in Bengaluru, monsoon slowdowns in Mumbai, rush hours in Delhi. "Send three riders to Koramangala at 7 p.m., one to Colaba at 9," it plans, matching riders to orders like a pro. It predicts peaks too—Saturday nights need 30% more hands—and optimizes routes to dodge delays. Zomato cuts delivery time by 25%—that's meals hot and happy—and saves 20% on fuel costs. Orders jump 30% because customers love the speed. Midsize hustle, massive win—AI turns chaos into cash.

Case Study 3: "Saree Serenity" – The Small Shop Social Star

Now, meet Neha, who runs "Saree Serenity," a tiny online shop selling sarees from her home in Lucknow. She's got INR 20,000 to spend monthly—every ad counts. She used to post on *Instagram*, hoping someone bites, but half her budget fizzled on ads no one saw. Then she grabs an AI tool from *Canva* (https://www.canva.com), a design app with a marketing twist.

This AI scans her posts—silk sarees get love, cotton lags—and checks who's clicking: mostly women 30-50, often liking festive pics. "Post silk saree ads Diwali week, target Uttar Pradesh," it says, crafting a campaign with pics and captions. Neha spends INR 10,000, hits the right crowd, and sales soar—50 sarees sold vs. 20 before, a 150% jump. Costs drop 20% (no wasted ads), profits climb INR 15,000 extra. Small shop, big win—AI makes her a social star.

How AI Drives These Wins?

These stories show AI flexing three profit-pumping muscles:

1. **Stock Smarts:** Walmart's AI nails inventory—20% less waste, 15% more sales—no overstock, no empty shelves.

2. **Delivery Dash:** Zomato's AI speeds orders—25% faster, 20% cheaper—hot food, happy wallets.
3. **Ad Accuracy:** Neha's AI targets buyers—150% sales lift, 20% cost cut—every rupee scores.

Here's the cash breakdown:

- **Time Saved:** Hours of planning—Walmart's stock, Zomato's routes, Neha's ads—shrink to minutes.
- **Costs Cut:** Waste (20%), fuel (20%), ad flops (20%)—savings stack up fast.
- **Profits Up:** Sales boosts (15%, 30%, 150%)—more buyers, more bucks.

Think about your own grind. Overstocked lately? Late deliveries? Ad cash down the drain? AI's the fix—big or small, it works.

Why This Matters to You?

These aren't just cool tales—they're blueprints. *Walmart* (https://www.walmart.com) shows scale, *Zomato* (https://www.zomato.com) proves hustle, Neha screams "you can too!" You don't need millions—tools from *Canva* (https://www.canva.com), *Google* (https://www.google.com), or suppliers fit any budget. Whether you're stocking a store, delivering goods, or posting ads, AI's your profit pal—saving time, cutting fat, growing cash.

The numbers don't lie. Walmart's millions, Zomato's 30%, Neha's INR 15,000—these are real wins. Less waste, more sales—it's money you can bank on. No tech degree—just plug in and profit.

A Peek Behind the Curtain (No Tech Talk, Promise!)

How's AI pulling this off? It's your eagle-eyed wingman. Watches sales (diapers vs. grills), tracks moves (traffic, orders), scans buzz (silk sarees)—then acts. Stock? "Order this." Routes? "Go here." Ads? "Hit them." It's not rocket science—it's a tool that's ace at spotting what wins, like you with endless eyes.

NINE

WHAT'S NEXT? – AI'S FUTURE IN BUSINESS

Introduction: Dreaming Big with AI

We've journeyed through how AI speeds up your daily grind, wows your customers, boosts your sales, streamlines your stuff, masters your money, builds your team, and delivers real wins for companies big and small. But here's the fun part: we're not done yet. The best is still ahead! Imagine a world where your business feels like it's reading your customers' minds, cutting waste like a pro, and growing bigger than you ever thought—all with AI as your trusty co-pilot. That's where we're headed, and this chapter's your sneak peek.

No techy stuff here—just a look at what's coming, explained like we're chatting over chai. We'll explore trends like shopping that's tailor-made for you, businesses going green with less mess, and how even your local kirana store could cash in someday. It's all about optimism—AI as your partner for growth—and profits that keep climbing as the future unfolds. Whether you're a shop owner, a manager, or dreaming of your own hustle, this is your chance to see what's possible. Let's peek into tomorrow and get excited!

Why the Future's Worth Caring About?

Running a business today is great, but staying ahead tomorrow? That's the golden ticket. The world's changing—customers want more, competition's tougher, and everyone's talking green. AI's not just a tool for now; it's your bridge to what's next. It's like having a crystal ball that doesn't just guess—it guides you to bigger wins. For non-tech folks like us, this isn't about sci-fi gadgets—it's about practical ideas that save time, make money, and keep your business buzzing. Let's see where AI's taking us, one profit-packed step at a time.

Trend 1: Shopping That's All About You – Personalization on Steroids

Imagine walking into a store—or clicking online—and it's like they've got you figured out. "Hey, you love blue kurtas—here's one cut just your size!" That's AI personalizing shopping even more, and it's coming fast. Picture Neha from "Saree Serenity" again, but five years from now. Her AI doesn't just suggest sarees—it knows Priya loves silk for weddings, Ravi digs cotton for work, and it tailors every ad, email, or pop-up to them. "Priya, silk saree, 15% off—perfect for Diwali!"

How's it work? AI watches what you buy, what you browse, even what you like on *Instagram* — then crafts offers so spot-on, you can't say no. Big players like *Amazon* are already there, but soon, your local boutique could do it too. More sales—say, 20-30% extra—because customers feel special, not spammed. Profit? Skyrocketing—less guesswork, more "add to cart." Could your shop make every customer feel VIP?

Trend 2: Going Green with Less Waste – AI as Your Eco-Pal

Businesses are under pressure to go green—less trash, less energy, happier planet. AI's stepping up to make it easy and profitable. Think of Vikram from "FreshBazaar" groceries. In the future, his AI doesn't just stock smart—it cuts waste to near zero. "Order 50 mangoes, not 60—rain's slowing sales," it says, or "Turn off fridges at 10 p.m.—sales drop then." It even predicts recycling—sell overripe fruit cheap before it rots.

This isn't just tree-hugging—it's cash-saving. Companies like *Walmart* (https://www.walmart.com) aim to slash waste 25% with AI, saving millions. Vikram could save 30% on spoilage—INR 50,000 yearly—while boosting his green cred, drawing eco-fans who spend more. Less waste, more profit—AI's your eco-pal making green mean gold. Ever thought about cutting trash and cashing in?

Trend 3: Smarter Stores, Even the Small Ones – AI for Everyone

AI's not staying with the big dogs — it's trickling down to your corner shop. Picture Arjun's "Bean Bliss Café" in 2030. His AI doesn't just pick coffee beans—it runs the show. "Today's hot—push iced lattes," it says, tweaking the menu on a digital board. It chats with customers via an app — "Want your usual?"—and schedules staff when it's busy. A kirana store could use it too — "Stock extra rice, festival's near," it nudges, all from a cheap phone app.

This levels the game. Small businesses grab tools from *Google* or *Canva*—no tech team needed—and see sales climb 15-20% with smarter moves. Profits grow because you're not guessing—you're knowing. Could your local hustle get that edge?

How These Trends Boost Profits?

These future tricks pack a profit punch:

1. **Personalization:** Tailored shopping lifts sales 20-30%—more buys, less flops.

2. **Green Gains:** Waste cuts (25-30%) save cash—INR 50,000 for Vikram, millions for Walmart—plus eco-appeal.
3. **Small Shop Smarts:** 15-20% sales bumps from sharp moves—no big budget, just big wins.

Here's the cash flow:

- **Time Saved:** Planning shrinks—minutes, not hours—freeing you for growth.
- **Costs Cut:** Less waste, less guesswork—savings stack up fast.
- **Revenue Up:** Smarter sales, happier buyers—profits soar as trends hit.

Think about your future. Want customers hooked? Waste slashed? AI's got your back, big or small.

Why This Matters to You?

You don't need to wait for 2030—this is starting now. Whether you're Neha selling sarees, Vikram stocking groceries, or Arjun brewing coffee, AI's future is your future. It's not about tech geekery—it's about growth you can grab. Tools from *Amazon*, *Google*, even free apps, are bringing this to you—cheap, easy, profit-ready. You're not a bystander; you're a player.

The profit potential's huge. A 20% sales lift, 30% waste cut—these aren't dreams; they're coming. AI's your partner, not a puzzle—helping you evolve, thrive, and cash in. Start small today, and you're ahead tomorrow.

A Peek Behind the Curtain (No Tech Talk, Promise!)

How's AI doing this? It's your eagle-eyed dreamer. Watches you (buys, likes), watches the world (weather, trends), then whispers winning moves. Personal? "She loves this—show it." Green? "Skip that—save it." Smart? "Push this—sell it." It's not sci-fi—it's a buddy who sees tomorrow and hands you the playbook.

TEN

YOUR TURN – HOW TO START USING AI IN YOUR BUSINESS

Introduction: Time to Take the Wheel

We've come a long way, haven't we? From speeding up your daily grind to wowing customers, boosting sales, streamlining operations, mastering money, building teams, seeing real wins, and peeking into the future—AI's been the star of the show. But here's the best part: this isn't just a spectator sport. It's your turn now! You don't need a tech degree or a fat wallet to jump in—AI's ready for you, right here, right now, to make your business sharper, faster, and more profitable.

In this final chapter, we're handing you the keys—practical, no-fuss steps to start using AI today. We'll point you to easy tools like chatbots from *Tidio* (https://www.tidio.com) or marketing magic from *Canva* (https://www.canva.com)—nothing complicated, just plug-and-play goodies you can try with a cup of chai in hand. Whether you're a shop owner, a freelancer, or dreaming of your own gig, this is about starting small, seeing the profit pop, and growing from there. No tech wizards required—just you, a little curiosity, and a big win waiting. Let's roll up our sleeves and get you started!

Why You Can Do This (Yes, YOU!)?

Maybe you're thinking, "AI sounds awesome, but I'm no geek—can I really pull this off?" Absolutely, yes! Everything we've talked about—Priya's chatbots, Neha's ads, Sanjay's forecasts—started with someone like you, not a scientist. AI's gone from rocket science to ready-made—tools are simple, cheap (sometimes free!), and built for regular folks. You don't need to code or crunch numbers—just click, play, and profit.

Here's the deal: businesses using AI today aren't special—they're just ahead. You've seen the wins—20% cost cuts, 30% sales boosts, happier teams. That's not magic; it's action. Start small, see the difference, and scale up—it's your business, your rules, your rewards. Let's break it down into steps even your grandma could follow, with tools you can grab right now.

Step 1: Start Small – Pick One Easy Win

Don't boil the ocean—pick one thing AI can fix today. Maybe it's a task you hate, like chasing emails, or a profit leak, like guessing stock. Here's how to start:

Automate Email Replies: Tired of typing "Thanks for your order!" a hundred times? Try *Tidio* (https://www.tidio.com)—a chatbot that answers for you. Set it up in 10 minutes—"Hi, your order's on the way!"—and watch it handle customers 24/7. Priya from Chapter 3 saw bookings jump 35% with this. Cost? Free to start, then INR 1,500/month if you love it.

Smart Social Ads: Wasting cash on ads no one sees? Use *Canva* (https://www.canva.com)'s AI—it picks who'll click based on likes (e.g., "Women 25-40 love sarees"). Neha from Chapter 8 boosted sales 150% this way. Free to try, INR 500/month for extras.

Track What Sells: Guessing stock like Sanjay's bakery? *Google Sheets* (https://www.google.com/sheets) has free AI add-ons—plug in sales, get "Order 50 cupcakes Saturday." His waste dropped 30%, profits rose 25%.

Pick one—emails, ads, stock—and test it. One hour, one tool, one win. See the profit nudge? That's your green light.

Step 2: See the Difference – Watch the Profits Pop

Once you've dipped your toe in, watch what happens. Let's say you're Arjun from "Bean Bliss Café" (Chapter 6). You try *Tidio* (https://www.tidio.com) for customer chats—"When's my latte ready?"—and it answers while you brew. Week one: you save an hour daily (INR 500 in time), take 10% more orders (INR 2,000 extra). That's INR 2,500 profit pop from one tweak—no tech fuss, just results.

Track it—write down time saved, costs cut, sales up. Neha's INR 15,000 jump, Vikram's 15% grocery lift—these started small too. Seeing the difference isn't just fun—it's fuel. When you spot INR 1,000 extra or an hour back, you'll itch to do more. That's AI working its magic, right in your hands.

Step 3: Scale Up – Grow Your Wins

Got a win? Double down! Start small, then build. Arjun loves *Tidio* (https://www.tidio.com), so he adds [Canva](https://www.canva.com) ads—"Iced lattes, 10% off!"—targeting hot-day fans. Sales climb 20% more (INR 4,000). Next, he tries *QuickBooks* (https://www.quickbooks.intuit.com) AI for budgets—"Order 10 kilos beans now"—cutting waste 20% (INR 1,000 saved). From one tool to three, his profit's up INR 5,000 monthly—INR 60,000 a year—without breaking a sweat.

Try this:

Customer Boost: Add *Mailchimp* (https://www.mailchimp.com)'s AI—send "Come back, 10% off!" like Sanjay's restaurant, upping repeat sales 40%.

Stock Smarts: Use *Shopify* (https://www.shopify.com)'s AI—predicts "Blue tees sell out," like Neha's kurtas, lifting sales 30%.

Team Help: Grab *Workplace* (https://www.workplace.com)'s AI—spots "Amit's stressed," cuts turnover 50% like Priya's café.

Start with one, stack another—each adds profit, no tech degree needed.

Tools to Try – Your AI Starter Kit

Here's your plug-and-play lineup—easy, affordable, profit-ready:

Tidio(https://www.tidio.com): Chatbots for customer chats—free to start, INR 1,500/month premium. (Time saved: 1 hr/day, Sales up: 10-35%)

Canva (https://www.canva.com): AI ads and designs—free basic, INR 500/month pro. (Sales up: 20-150%, Costs down: 20%)

Google Sheets (https://www.google.com/sheets): Free AI add-ons for sales tracking—INR 0. (Waste down: 20-30%, Sales up: 25%)

Mailchimp (https://www.mailchimp.com): AI email offers—free to 500 contacts, INR 1,000/month more. (Repeat sales: 40%)

QuickBooks (https://www.quickbooks.intuit.com): Budget AI—INR 1,500/month. (Mistakes down: 20%, Profits up: 20%)

No coding—just sign up, click, go. Pick one today, profit tomorrow.

Why This Matters to You?

This isn't for tech nerds—it's for YOU. Shop owner? Freelancer? Dreamer? AI's your shortcut—less grind, more gain. You've seen it—Priya's INR 15,000, Sanjay's 25%, Walmart's millions—all from starting somewhere. You don't need a big budget or a PhD—just a phone, a tool, and a spark. One step saves an hour, makes INR 1,000—scale it, and you're rolling in it.

The profit's real. A 20% boost here, 30% there—it adds up. You're not watching from the sidelines—you're playing to win. AI's your partner, not a puzzle—empowering you to grow, no tech fuss needed.

Your Call to Action: Try It, See It, Grow It

Here's your challenge: pick one tool today—*Tidio* (https://www.tidio.com), Canva (www.canva.com), whatever clicks. Try it this week—set up a chatbot, run an ad, track a sale. See the difference—time saved, cash up—then scale it. Arjun started with INR 2,500; you could too. One move, one win, then more—your business, your profits, your future.

You've got the map—now take the wheel. Try it, see the profit pop, and grow from there. No excuses—AI's waiting, and so's your next big win. Go for it!

A Peek Behind the Curtain (No Tech Talk, Promise!)

How's AI so easy? It's your plug-in pal—watches what you do (sales, clicks), learns fast, acts simple. Chatbots? "Answer this." Ads? "Show these folks." Budgets? "Spend here." It's not rocket science—it's a buddy who does the grunt work so you shine.

Conclusion: Your Ai Journey Starts Here

And there you have it, folks—we've made it to the end of our adventure together! From the moment we cracked open "What is AI, and Why Should You Care?" to now, we've seen how Artificial Intelligence isn't some distant tech dream—it's a real, right-now tool that's changing businesses for the better. We've walked through speeding up the daily grind, delighting customers, pumping up sales, streamlining operations, mastering money, building killer teams, celebrating real wins, peeking into the future, and finally, putting the keys in your hands. If there's one thing I hope you take away, it's this: AI's not just for the big shots—it's for YOU, and it's ready to make your profits pop.

Let's rewind for a sec. Remember Priya's coffee shop cutting waste with a simple app? Or Neha's saree sales soaring 150% with a smart ad tweak? How about Zomato zipping food faster or Walmart saving millions on stock? These aren't fairy tales—they're proof. AI's already out there saving hours, slashing costs by 20-30%, and boosting sales from 15% to triple digits. And the best part? You don't need to be a tech whiz to join the party—just a spark of curiosity and a willingness to try.

This book's been about keeping it real—no geeky jargon, just stories and steps for folks like us. Whether you're a café owner juggling beans, a freelancer chasing gigs, or a dreamer sketching your next big thing, AI's your buddy. It's the extra pair of hands that says, "I've got this—go grow your business." We've seen it work across the board—operations, customer service, marketing, manufacturing, finance, HR—and it's not stopping. The future's bright, with personalized shopping, greener wins, and smarter small shops, all piling up more cash for those who grab it.

So, where do you go from here? Simple: start. Flip back to Chapter 10, pick a tool—Tidio for chats, Canva for ads, QuickBooks for budgets—and give it a whirl. Start small—maybe automate an email or track a sale—and watch the difference. An hour saved, INR 1,000 extra—it's not just numbers; it's momentum. Scale it up, and soon you're the one with a story—your own 20% profit boost or a team that's humming. You've got the map; now take the first step.

Writing this book has been a blast for me—imagining your wins, sharing these tales, and knowing you're out there ready to make it happen. This isn't goodbye—it's "see you at the top." AI's not a mystery anymore—it's your ticket to less hassle and more hustle. So, close this book, grab that tool, and start today. Your business deserves it, your profits demand it, and you've got it in you to make it big. Here's to your AI journey—let's cash in and keep climbing!

Closing Note: The Journey's Yours

That's it, folks—your roadmap to AI profits. From basics to future, you've seen it work—now make it yours. Start small, dream big, cash in. You're not just a reader—you're a doer. Grab a tool, try it today, and watch your business soar. The profits? They're waiting for you!